Song for the Journey

30 Days of Devotions

Karen Kazimer Shockley

Karen's Words

Contents

Introduction

Some songs are sung on bright days, when the sky is clear and our hearts feel light.
But the truest songs—the ones God treasures most—are sung through tears, through waiting, through quiet faithfulness.

This little book was born from that kind of song.

I have watched love in many forms: in mothers who prayed through sleepless nights, in fathers who worked faithfully, in children who forgave quickly, in families who stayed together when life grew hard. I have seen love sing through illness, through loss, through uncertainty, and through joy.

And I have learned something simple but beautiful:

Love sings on.

It sings in kitchens while supper cooks.
It sings in whispered bedtime prayers.
It sings in hospital rooms, church pews, and long car rides.
It sings when no one applauds.

Like the real-life couple who kept singing in small halls in the story behind *Song Sung Blue*, like Mother Rachel standing strong in Haven Ridge when tragedy came, like families everywhere who hold on to faith—true love does not stop when life gets difficult. It grows deeper.

This 30-day devotional is an invitation to slow down and listen to that song.

Each day offers:

• A King James Version Scripture
• A short reflection

• A four-line prayer
• A simple activity

These moments are meant to be gentle companions in your mornings, evenings, or quiet afternoons. You can read them alone, with your spouse, with your children, or with a dear friend.

My prayer is that these pages will help you:

• Find peace in hard seasons
• Strengthen your marriage and family

To My Family

Whose love has been the music of my life—through laughter, through tears, through ordinary days and unexpected storms.

To mothers who pray in quiet rooms,
fathers who work faithfully,
children who forgive quickly,
and families everywhere who hold on to hope.

To my dear brother Steven,
one of the kindest hearts I have ever known,
always ready to help, always loving,
a reminder that gentle goodness changes the world.

To every reader searching for comfort,
for peace, for faith that lasts longer than fear. This book is for you.
Because love is not measured by applause or ease,
but by faithfulness.

As Scripture says, "Charity suffereth long, and is kind... beareth all things, believeth all things, hopeth all things, endureth all things."
—1 Corinthians 13:4,7 Love endures.

Through loss and waiting, through illness and uncertainty, God's promise still sings over us: "Weeping may endure for a night, but joy cometh in the morning."
—Psalm 30:5 Joy returns.

And through every season of life, we remember: "I will sing of the mercies of the Lord for ever: with my mouth will I make known thy faithfulness to all generations."
—Psalm 89:1 God's love sings on.

This book is dedicated to the quiet heroes of faith—
the ones who forgive, who pray, who keep loving,
who hold families together when life feels fragile.

May the Lord bless you and keep you.

May He fill your home with peace.

May He strengthen your heart with hope. And may your life become a song of love that never ends.

With gratitude and prayer,

Karen Kazimer Shockley

Cross and Prayerbook - Wisdom for Leadership

Day 1 – Love Begins with a Song

Psalm 95:1 – "O come, let us sing unto the Lord: let us make a joyful noise to the rock of our salvation."

Every love story begins with hope. Before vows are spoken, before children are born, before trials come, love starts quietly—with trust, with kindness, with praise. The happiest families I have known began not with perfect circumstances, but with hearts turned toward God. They prayed together in kitchens, sang hymns on Sundays, and whispered thanks even in hard times.

Praise sets the tone for love. When we thank God for one another, we remember that love is a gift, not something we own. Like Mother Rachel and Father Daniel in Haven Ridge, love grows stronger when rooted in gratitude. They faced storms, yet their home still echoed with song.

You don't need a beautiful voice. God hears the whisper of a thankful heart. When you sing, even softly, your worries loosen, your hope rises, and your love deepens. Begin today with praise—for your spouse, your children, your dear brother Steven who always showed kindness, and the blessings you may have overlooked.

Love begins with a song of gratitude. And when we start there, our journey is filled with peace.

Prayer:

Lord, teach my heart to sing in gratitude.
Fill my home with songs of hope and peace.
Help me begin each love story with praise.
Let my life be music that honors You.

Activity:

Play one worship song this morning.

Day 2 – Singing Through Hard Times

Psalm 30:5 -- "For his anger endureth but a moment; in his favour is life: weeping may endure for a night, but joy cometh in the

morning."

Reflection:

Even faithful couples face storms. Illness comes. Jobs change. Children struggle. Hearts grow weary. Yet love that keeps singing through hardship becomes stronger than before. Faith does not promise an easy road, but it promises God's presence.

In Haven Ridge, families gathered when tragedy came. They prayed together, cried together, and sang together. Their voices were not perfect—but their faith was real. Singing reminds us that sorrow is not the end of our story. God's love carries us through the night until joy returns.

When you feel overwhelmed, try a small song of trust. Whisper a hymn while washing dishes. Play worship music while driving. Let praise fill your home like light through a window. It changes the atmosphere, softens anger, and gives courage.

Prayer:

Give me courage in quiet trials, Lord.
Help me trust You when storms arise.
Remind me joy comes in the morning.
Keep our love strong in hard seasons.

Activity:

Write one blessing from a hard season.

Day 3 – Love That Always Listens

James 1:19 -- "Wherefore, my beloved brethren, let every man be swift to hear, slow to speak, slow to wrath:"

Love listens more than it speaks. In a noisy world, listening has become rare, yet it is one of the greatest gifts we can offer. When we listen, we say, "You matter to me."

Children feel safe when parents listen. Spouses feel valued when heard without interruption. Friends find comfort when someone sits quietly beside them. Even God listens to our prayers with patient love.

Think of Jesus listening to hurting people. He stopped, looked into their eyes, and heard their hearts. We can do the same in our homes. Turn off the phone. Sit close. Give ten minutes of full attention. You may hear worries you didn't know existed—or joys waiting to be shared.

Listening also teaches humility. We learn that others carry burdens we cannot see. Kindness grows when understanding grows. In families like yours, where love is steady, listening becomes a daily act of grace.

Tonight, listen to someone you love. Listen without fixing, correcting, or rushing. Just listen.

Because when love listens, hearts heal—and the song of peace grows louder.

Prayer:

Help me hear my family's needs today.
Quiet my words so I can listen well.
Give me patience and gentle understanding.
Let love guide every conversation.

Activity:

Give someone 10 minutes of full attention.

Day 4 – Faithful in Small Places

Scripture:

Luke 16:10 -- "He that is faithful in that which is least is faithful also in much: and he that is unjust in the least is unjust also in much."

Reflection:

True love grows in ordinary days. It lives in packed lunches, washed socks, bedtime prayers, and quiet encouragement. The world celebrates big moments, but God treasures small faithfulness.

A mother rocking a baby at midnight sings a holy song. A father fixing a tire in the rain sings another. Children helping with chores, grandparents reading stories, friends sending kind notes —these are melodies of love.

Jesus taught that faithfulness in little things leads to greater blessings. When we do small acts with care, we build trust, kindness, and peace. Homes become warm places where love feels safe.

Prayer:

Bless my daily work at home, Lord.
Help me serve with a cheerful heart.
Make small tasks acts of holy love.
Let faith grow in ordinary days.

Activity:

Do one unseen act of kindness.

Day 5 – Harmony in Every Marriage

Colossians 3:14 -- "And above all these things put on charity, which is the bond of perfectness."

Love binds hearts like harmony binds music. Marriage is not two perfect voices singing alone—it is two imperfect voices learning one song. Sometimes the notes are uncertain. Sometimes rhythms clash. But with patience and prayer, harmony grows.

Marriage is built in ordinary days: sharing worries, forgiving mistakes, laughing at small joys. When couples pray together, they remember that God is the center of their home. His love keeps them steady when emotions rise.

Think of couples who stayed faithful through hardship. Their secret was not perfection—it was commitment. They chose kindness when angry, gentleness when tired, hope when afraid.

Harmony takes listening, humility, and forgiveness. It means saying "I'm sorry," and "I forgive you," and "Let's try again." It means cheering for each other's dreams and carrying each other's burdens.

When two hearts trust God together, love becomes stronger than storms. Their home fills with peace, like a hymn sung softly at sunset.

Marriage harmony grows slowly, but it grows beautifully. And when God leads, love sings in perfect time.

Prayer:

Unite our hearts, dear Lord, in harmony.
Teach us kindness in every moment.
Let forgiveness heal our differences.
Keep our love steady and strong.

Activity:

Pray with your spouse or friend.

Day 6 – Joy in Motherhood

Scripture:

Proverbs 31:28 -- "Her children arise up, and call her blessed; her husband also, and he praiseth her."

Reflection:

A mother's love sings in quiet sacrifices. She wakes early, stays late, prays often, and worries deeply. Yet her love shines in small acts—packing lunches, kissing scraped knees, whispering bedtime prayers.

Motherhood is holy work. It shapes hearts, teaches kindness, and plants seeds of faith. Children remember gentle words long after toys are forgotten. They remember stories, songs, and hugs.

Even when mothers feel unnoticed, God sees their devotion. He hears their prayers for children far away. He knows their hopes and fears. He blesses their patience.

Think of mothers who influenced your life—maybe your own mother, a teacher, or a church friend. Their love was steady and faithful. Like Rachel in Haven Ridge, mothers carry families through storms. Today, thank God for mothers everywhere. Pray for strength for those who are tired, comfort for those who grieve, and joy for those watching children grow.

Motherhood is a quiet song of love. And through generations, its melody continues.

Prayer:

Strengthen mothers everywhere, Lord.
Bless their quiet sacrifices of love.
Give them rest, hope, and joy.
Let their children rise and call them blessed.

Activity:

Write a note to your children.

Day 7 – Singing on Each Sunday

Scripture:

Hebrews 10:25 -- "Not forsaking the assembling of ourselves to-gether, as the manner of some is; but exhorting one another: and so much the more, as ye see the day approaching."

Reflection:

Worship together strengthens love. When families gather in church, they share faith, hope, and joy. Singing hymns side by side reminds us that we are not alone.

Church songs carry memories. We remember childhood pews, Christmas choirs, Easter mornings, and voices raised in praise. These moments become anchors in hard times.

When children see parents worship, they learn faith is real. When couples pray together, trust deepens. When friends sing together, community grows.

Even if voices are soft or uncertain, God hears sincere praise. Worship fills hearts with peace and homes with kindness. It reminds us of God's promises and gives courage for the week ahead.

Think of a hymn that comforts you. Sing it today. Let it echo in your home. Let it carry your worries to God.

Because when we worship together, love grows stronger. Faith becomes steady. And our hearts learn a song that lasts forever.

Prayer:

Bless our church family, Lord.
Let us worship with joyful hearts.
Fill our songs with faith and unity.
Draw us closer together in You.

Activity:

Sing a hymn together.

Day 8 – Forgiveness Restores the Song

Scripture:

Ephesians 4:32 -- "And be ye kind one to another, tenderhearted, forgiving one another, even as God for Christ's sake hath forgiven you."

Forgiveness resets the melody of love. Hurt is part of every relationship, but bitterness is a choice. When we forgive, we free our hearts from anger and open the door to peace.

Forgiveness does not ignore wrong—it chooses mercy. It remembers how much God has forgiven us. Jesus showed love even when hurt deeply. His example teaches us compassion.

In families, forgiveness heals wounds quickly. Children learn grace when parents forgive. Couples grow closer when pride gives way to kindness. Friends rebuild trust when apologies are sincere.

Think of someone you need to forgive. Pray for strength. Speak gently. Take a small step. You may feel peace sooner than expected.

Forgiveness brings harmony back into homes. It softens hearts and restores hope. Like a broken instrument repaired, love can sing again.

Prayer:

Soften my heart, dear Lord.
Help me forgive as You forgive me.
Restore the melody of peace.
Let love begin again today.

Activity:

Apologize where needed.

Day 9 – Love in Loss

Scripture:

Matthew 5:4 -- "Blessed are they that mourn: for they shall be comforted."

Reflection:

God sings comfort over grieving hearts. Loss touches every family—through illness, distance, disappointment, or death. Grief is heavy, yet God stays close.

In sorrow, we remember love. We remember laughter, kindness, and shared moments. Memories become treasures. Love does not disappear—it changes form.

Think of someone you miss. Perhaps a parent, a friend, or a loved one like those we hold dear in family stories. Their love still lives in us. God keeps their memory safe.

In hard seasons, prayer brings peace. Church friends bring comfort. Scripture brings hope. God promises that joy will come again.

It is okay to cry. It is okay to remember. It is okay to hope. Love and grief often walk together.

Trust that God holds your heart gently. He understands sorrow. He gives strength day by day.

Even in loss, love sings softly. And one day, joy will return like sunrise after night.

Prayer:

Hold those who mourn, dear Lord.
Comfort hearts that feel alone.
Send hope like morning light.
Let Your love bring healing.

Activity:

Call someone hurting.

Day 10 – Kindness Is Music

Scripture:

Proverbs 16:24 -- "Pleasant words are as an honeycomb, sweet to the soul, and health to the bones."

Reflection:

Gentle words are healing songs. Kindness can change a whole day, a whole family, even a whole life. A smile, a compliment, a note, a helping hand—these are melodies of love.

Kindness shows Christ's heart. Jesus spoke gently, healed patiently, and welcomed the weary. We can do the same in our homes.

Speak softly when angry. Encourage when someone feels unsure. Thank those who help you. Notice small efforts. Kindness grows where gratitude lives.

Think of someone who was kind to you when you needed it most. Maybe your brother Steven with his generous heart, always ready to help. Kindness leaves lasting memories.

Today, give kindness freely. It costs little but gives much. It softens hard days, strengthens friendships, and fills homes with peace.

Kindness is music God loves to hear. And when we practice it daily, love sings beautifully in our lives.

Prayer:

Make my words sweet, Lord.
Let kindness shape my speech.
Help me lift weary hearts.
Let my voice be gentle music.

Activity:

Compliment three people.

Day 11 – Love That Works Hard

Scripture:

Galatians 6:9 -- And let us not be weary in well doing: for in due season we shall reap, if we faint not."

Reflection:

Love is not only a feeling—it is faithful work. It shows up in early mornings, late nights, long drives, and quiet prayers. It fixes broken toys, cooks meals, listens to worries, and keeps going when no one notices.

God honors this steady love. Scripture reminds us not to grow weary in doing good. Each act of care is a seed planted in faith. Over time, those seeds grow into trust, security, and peace within a family.

Think of parents who labored quietly, or spouses who stayed faithful through hard years. Their love may not have been dramatic, but it was strong. Like Father Daniel working for his family, or Rachel praying through storms, faithful love builds homes that endure.

When you feel tired, remember your work matters. Your kindness matters. Your prayers matter. God sees every sacrifice.

Today, finish one task you've been putting off. Offer it as an act of love. Even small efforts can bless someone deeply.

Love that works hard becomes love that lasts. And its steady rhythm keeps the song of hope alive.

Prayer:

Lord, renew my strength when I grow tired.
Help me love faithfully in daily work.
Give me patience in small frustrations.
Let perseverance grow into joy.

Activity:

Finish one delayed task.

Day 12 – Singing Through the Storm

Scripture:

Psalm 30:5 -- "For his anger endureth but a moment; in his favour is life: weeping may endure for a night, but joy cometh in the morning."

Reflection:

Storms come to every life. Illness, worry, disappointment, and loss can shake even strong faith. Yet love that keeps singing through storms becomes deeper and stronger than before.

Think of a couple standing together in hard times—holding hands, praying quietly, trusting God. They may not feel brave, but they stay faithful. Like the little tribute band behind *Song Sung Blue*, they keep singing even without applause. Their love is steady because it rests in God.

When storms come, try a small song of faith. Whisper a hymn while folding laundry. Play worship music while driving. Let praise remind you that God is near. Music has a way of lifting sorrow and calming fear.

Remember past storms God carried you through. Those memories become anchors. They remind us that hardship does not last forever.

Even when tears fall, hope remains. God walks with us through dark valleys and leads us into light again.

Keep singing through the storm. Love grows stronger, faith grows deeper, and joy returns with morning.

Prayer:

Help me stay faithful when no one sees.
Give me courage when applause is gone.
Teach me to sing through quiet trials.
Let love endure through every storm.

Activity:

Sing a hymn tonight.

Day 13 – Hope Returns

Jeremiah 29:11 -- "For I know the Reflections that I think toward you, saith the Lord, Reflections of peace, and not of evil, to give you an expected end."

Reflection:

God writes beautiful endings. Even when life feels uncertain, His plans are filled with peace and purpose. Hope may seem small at times, but it is never gone.

Think of seeds buried in winter soil. They look lifeless, yet spring comes. In the same way, God grows hope quietly inside us. Hard seasons prepare us for new blessings.

Perhaps you have waited for an answer, healing, or reconciliation. Waiting is painful, but God uses it to strengthen faith. Families in Haven Ridge learned patience through trials, yet their love became deeper because of it.

Look for signs of hope today—a kind word, a sunrise, a child's laugh, a prayer answered. These are reminders of God's care.

Write a prayer for the future. Give your worries to God. Trust His timing, even when you cannot see the whole path.

Hope is not wishful thinking. It is confidence in God's love. And when hope returns, our hearts begin to sing again.

Prayer:

Fill my heart with hope today, Lord.
Remind me You write good endings.
Help me trust Your perfect timing.
Let joy bloom again in my life.

Activity:

Write a future prayer.

Day 14 – Love Is Patient

Scripture:

1 Corinthians 13:4 -- "Charity suffereth long, and is kind; charity envieth not; charity vaunteth not itself, is not puffed up,"

Reflection:

Patience keeps the rhythm of love. Without it, relationships stumble. With it, they grow strong and peaceful.

Patience means waiting kindly. It means speaking gently when irritated. It means remembering that everyone is learning and growing. Children need patience as they mature. Spouses need patience as they face stress. Friends need patience when they struggle.

Jesus showed patience with His disciples again and again. He taught slowly, corrected gently, and loved faithfully. We can follow His example in our homes.

Think of a moment when someone was patient with you. Perhaps a teacher, parent, or friend. Their kindness gave you courage to keep trying. Patience is a gift that blesses both giver and receiver.

Today, pause before speaking. Breathe. Pray. Choose calm words. Offer understanding instead of anger.

Patience turns arguments into conversations and mistakes into lessons. It keeps love steady through hard moments.

When patience guides us, our homes become peaceful places where love's song can grow stronger every day.

Prayer:

Slow my spirit, gentle Lord.
Teach me calm in waiting moments.
Help me answer with kindness.
Let patience keep our love strong.

Activity:

Wait without complaining.

Day 15 – Love Celebrates Small Wins

Scripture:

Zechariah 4:10 -- "For who hath despised the day of small things? for they shall rejoice..."

Reflection:

Rejoice in little victories. God often works through small beginnings. A child learning to read, Luke learning soccer in your stories, a new job, a healed friendship—these moments deserve celebration.

When we notice small blessings, gratitude grows. Families become happier when they cheer for each other's efforts. Children feel encouraged. Spouses feel appreciated. Friends feel valued.

God delights in small progress. He sees every step of growth. No effort made in love is wasted.

Think of a tiny success today. Maybe you finished a chore, spoke kindly, or kept a promise. Thank God for it. Share joy with someone.

Celebrating small wins keeps hope alive. It reminds us that change is possible and God is working quietly.

Light a candle. Say a prayer. Smile together. Let your home echo with gratitude.

Because love grows stronger when joy is shared—and even small victories become songs of praise.

Prayer:

Help me notice little blessings today.
Teach me joy in tiny victories.
Let me cheer for those I love.
Fill our home with grateful praise.

Activity:

Celebrate one small success.

Day 16 – Love Teaches

Scripture:

Deuteronomy 6:7 -- "And thou shalt teach them diligently unto thy children, and shalt talk of them when thou sittest in thine house..."

Reflection:

Love teaches gently and faithfully. Parents teach children with bedtime stories, prayer, and example. Grandparents teach wisdom through memories. Teachers shape hearts with patience.

God tells us to teach His words to our children. Not only with books, but with kindness, honesty, and faith. Children watch how we live. They learn forgiveness by seeing forgiveness, generosity by seeing generosity.

Think of someone who taught you faith. Perhaps a Sunday school teacher, your mother, or a pastor. Their love shaped your life.

Today, teach something good. Read a Bible story. Pray aloud. Show kindness. Answer questions with patience.

Teaching love is not about perfection. It is about consistency. Small lessons repeated daily grow into strong faith.

When love teaches, generations are blessed. And long after we are gone, our lessons continue to sing.

Prayer:

Guide my children's hearts, dear Lord.
Help me teach with wisdom and grace.
Let bedtime prayers plant faith.
May our home be a school of love.

Activity:

Read one Bible story aloud.

Day 17 – Singing in Gratitude

Scripture:

1 Thessalonians 5:18 -- "In every thing give thanks: for this is the will of God in Christ Jesus concerning you."

Reflection:

Gratitude sweetens love. When we thank God for our blessings, our hearts grow lighter and kinder. Complaints fade. Joy returns.

Look around your home. Notice simple gifts: a warm meal, a child's laughter, a friend's call, a peaceful evening. These are treasures.

Gratitude changes perspective. Instead of focusing on what is missing, we see what God has given. Families who practice gratitude become happier and more loving.

Write five thank-yous today. Thank God. Thank someone you love. Thank someone who helped you. Gratitude spreads like sunshine.

Think of blessings from the past year. Even hard times may hold lessons. God's care is always present, even when hidden.

Prayer:

Thank You for this precious day.
Help me see Your gifts around me.
Fill my words with thankful praise.
Let gratitude brighten my love.

Activity:

Write five thank-you notes.

Day 18 – Love Shows Up

Scripture:

Romans 12:10 -- "Be kindly affectioned one to another with brotherly love; in honour preferring one another;"

Reflection:

Love shows up in quiet, ordinary ways. It is not always dramatic or noticed, yet it is deeply felt. Love is sitting beside someone who is worried, attending a child's game after a long day, calling a friend who is lonely, or bringing soup to a neighbor. These small acts say, "You matter to me."

Showing up is a choice. It means giving time when we feel busy, patience when we feel tired, and kindness when we feel stressed. God shows up for us every day—with mercy in the morning and comfort at night. When we show up for others, we reflect His love.

Think of someone who showed up for you when you needed it most. Perhaps your kind brother Steven with his ready heart to help. Those moments stay with us forever. Presence is one of love's greatest gifts.

Today, ask yourself where love is calling you to show up. A visit, a note, a prayer, a listening ear—these are simple but powerful. When love shows up faithfully, homes grow warmer, friendships grow deeper, and God's peace fills our lives.

Prayer:

Help me be present for my family.
Teach me to listen with care.
Give me time for what matters most.
Let my love be seen in action.

Activity:

Attend a child's event or call family.

Day 19 – Love Encourages

Scripture:

Hebrews 3:13 -- "But exhort one another daily… lest any of you be hardened through the deceitfulness of sin."

Reflection:

Encouragement is a gentle song that lifts weary hearts. A few kind words can change someone's whole day. When we encourage others, we remind them of their strength, their purpose, and God's faithfulness.

Children blossom when praised for effort. Spouses feel valued when their work is noticed. Friends gain courage when someone believes in them. Encouragement builds confidence and spreads hope.

Think of someone who encouraged you when you doubted yourself. Maybe a parent, teacher, pastor, or dear friend. Their words still echo in your heart. Like Steven's kindness, encouragement leaves lasting light.

Today, choose to encourage someone. Send a message. Speak gratitude. Tell someone you are proud of them. Pray for their dreams. Your words may be exactly what they need.

Encouragement does not need grand speeches. It needs sincerity. When we uplift one

Prayer:

Make me uplifting to weary hearts.
Help me speak hope to others.
Let my words build faith and courage.
Use me to bring comfort today

Activity:

Send one encouraging text.

Day 20 – Love Is Gentle

Philippians 4:5 -- "Let your moderation be known unto all men.
The Lord is at hand."

(Moderation here means gentleness.)

Reflection:

Gentleness keeps harmony in every relationship. Loud anger may win an argument, but gentle words win hearts. When we speak softly, we show respect and patience. When we pause before reacting, we protect love.

Jesus showed gentleness to children, to sinners, to the hurting. He did not crush broken hearts—He healed them. We can follow His example in our homes.

Gentleness means choosing kindness when tired, calm when frustrated, grace when disappointed. It means remembering that every person carries hidden worries.

Think of someone whose gentle spirit comforted you—perhaps a grandmother, teacher, or friend. Their kindness stayed with you. Gentleness leaves lasting peace.

Today, slow your voice. Smile when irritated. Pray before speaking. Choose patience instead of harshness.

Gentleness makes homes safe places where love can grow. And when gentleness leads us, our lives become songs of peace.

Prayer:

Calm my voice, dear Lord.
Teach me gentleness in speech.
Help me show kindness in conflict.
Let peace guide every word.

Activity:

Speak softly today.

Day 21 – Singing in Faith

Scripture:

Psalm 28:7 -- "The Lord is my strength and my shield; my heart trusted in him, and I am helped..."

Reflection:

Faith sings even when answers are not clear. Trusting God means believing His love is steady, even in uncertainty.

There are seasons when we cannot see the path ahead. Yet God walks with us. Like families in Haven Ridge who trusted through tragedy, faith carried them forward.

Faith grows in small steps—daily prayer, Scripture reading, quiet trust. Each act of faith strengthens our hearts.

Write one worry on paper. Give it to God. Pray over it. Trust His wisdom.

Faith is not ignoring fear—it is trusting God despite fear.

And when we sing in faith, hope grows stronger than worry.

Prayer:

Increase my faith for tomorrow.
Help me trust when I cannot see.
Remind me You hold our future.
Let my heart rest in You.

Activity:

Write a worry, give it to God.

Day 22 – Love Serves

Scripture:

Mark 10:45 -- "For even the Son of man came not to be ministered unto, but to minister…"

Reflection:

Service is love in action. Jesus came not to be served, but to serve. When we help others, we reflect His heart.

Service can be simple: cooking a meal, making a call, helping a neighbor, praying for a friend. These acts bring comfort and hope.

Think of someone who served you quietly. Maybe your brother Steven offering help without being asked. Service leaves deep gratitude.

Today, do one act of service. Offer it to God.

Service brings joy because love was meant to be shared.

And when we serve others, love sings through our hands.

Prayer:

Make me willing to serve today.
Help me give without complaint.
Teach me joy in helping others.
Let service become my song.

Activity:

Do one chore for someone else.

Day 23 – Love Laughs

Proverbs 17:22 -- "A merry heart doeth good like a medicine: but a broken spirit drieth the bones."

Reflection:

A merry heart brings healing. Laughter is a gift from God. It lightens burdens, strengthens friendships, and fills homes with joy.

Families that laugh together stay close. Funny stories, shared memories, silly moments—these become treasures.

Even in hard times, laughter reminds us that hope remains. It softens grief and brings comfort.

Think of a joyful memory with someone you love. Smile. Thank God for it.

Today, share a funny story, play a game, watch something gentle together.

Laughter is a song of joy that blesses hearts.

And when love laughs, peace grows stronger.

Prayer:

Fill our home with holy laughter.
Let joy heal weary hearts.
Help us smile through worries.
Make happiness a family gift.

Activity:

Watch something funny together.

Day 24 – Love Remembers

Scripture:

Psalm 77:11-- "I will remember the works of the Lord: surely I will remember thy wonders of old."

Reflection:

Remembering past blessings strengthens faith. When we look

back, we see God's faithfulness clearly.

Think of people who shaped your life—parents, friends, pastors, maybe your dear brother Steven with his generous spirit. Their love lives on in memories.

Write down a special memory today. Thank God for it.

Remembering helps us trust God for tomorrow.

Love remembers kindness, forgiveness, laughter, and prayer.

And those memories keep the song of love alive.

Prayer:

Thank You for yesterday's blessings.
Help me remember Your goodness.
Let memories strengthen my faith.
Keep gratitude alive in my heart.

Activity:

Write a memory of time with a friend.

Day 25 – Love Prays Together

Matthew 18:20 -- "For where two or three are gathered together in my name, there am I in the midst of them."

Reflection:

Prayer strengthens families. When we pray together, hearts unite.

Worries feel lighter. Hope grows stronger.

Couples who pray together stay close. Parents who pray with children plant seeds of faith.

Prayer does not need perfect words. Honest hearts are enough.

Tonight, hold hands and pray aloud. Thank God for blessings. Ask for guidance.

Prayer invites God into our homes.

And when families pray together, love sings in harmony.

Prayer:

Draw our family close in prayer.
Let our voices rise together.
Teach us faith in hard moments.
Keep our home rooted in You.

Activity:

Pray aloud tonight.

Day 26 – Love Trusts God

Scripture:

Proverbs 3:5 -- "Trust in the Lord with all thine heart; and lean not unto thine own understanding."

Reflection:

Trust in the Lord with all your heart. God sees what we cannot. He guides with wisdom.

Trusting God means releasing fear and believing His plan is good.

Think of times God helped you unexpectedly. Remember His faithfulness.

Today, give one fear to God. Pray. Trust.

Love trusts God because His love never fails.

And trust fills hearts with peace.

Prayer:

I trust You with my future, Lord.
Help me release my fears.
Teach me to lean on Your wisdom.
Let peace guard my heart.

Activity:

Release one fear.

Day 27 – Love Persists

Scripture:

Galatians 6:9 -- And let us not be weary in well doing: for in due season we shall reap, if we faint not."

Reflection:

Love does not quit. It stays faithful through tired days and hard seasons.

Persistence means choosing kindness again and again. It means forgiving repeatedly and believing in better days.

Think of couples who stayed together through hardship. Their love grew deeper.

Write reasons you love your family today.

Persistence strengthens faith.

And love that endures becomes a song of hope.

Prayer:

Help me keep loving without quitting.
Strengthen me when I feel weak.
Teach me endurance in trials.
Let faith carry me forward.

Activity:

Write why you love your family.

Day 28 – Love Comforts

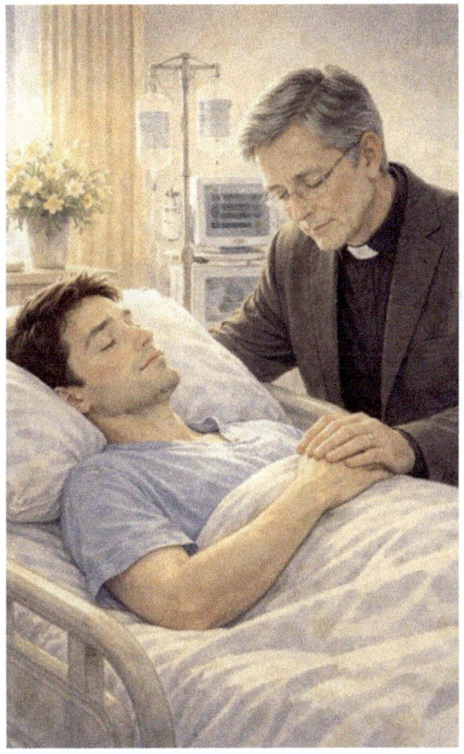

Scripture:

2 Corinthians 1:4 -- "Who comforteth us in all our tribulation, that we may be able to comfort them which are in any trouble..."

Reflection:

Comforting others reflects God's care. A gentle word, a hug, a prayer—these heal hurting hearts.

When someone grieves, presence matters more than answers.

Call someone hurting today. Pray for them.

God comforts us so we can comfort others.

And love becomes a shelter for weary hearts.

Prayer:

Use me to comfort hurting hearts.
Give me gentle words to share.
Let kindness bring healing.
Make me a messenger of peace.

Activity:

Send a sympathy card.

Day 29 – Love Rejoices

Scripture:

Romans 12:15 -- "Rejoice with them that do rejoice, and weep with them that weep."

Reflection:

Rejoice with those who rejoice. Celebrate others' blessings. Joy shared becomes joy multiplied.

When friends succeed, cheer for them. When children grow, celebrate.

Gratitude removes jealousy and grows love.

Today, congratulate someone sincerely.

Love rejoices because God is good.

And joy keeps love singing.

Prayer:

Help me celebrate others' blessings.
Remove envy from my heart.
Teach me joy in shared happiness.
Let love rejoice in truth.

Activity:

Congratulate someone.

<h1 style="text-align:center">Day30 – Song for the
Journey Forever</h1>

Psalm 89:1 -- "I will sing of the mercies of the Lord for ever: with my mouth will I make known thy faithfulness to all generations."

Reflection:

True love never stops singing. God's love lasts beyond every season.

Through joy and sorrow, through youth and age, through life and eternity—His love remains.

Think of heaven's songs waiting for us.

Sing today. Pray today. Love today.

Because love sings on forever.

And with God, our hearts will sing too.

Prayer:

Let my life be a song of love.
Help me praise You every day.
Keep faith alive in my home.
May love sing on forever.

Activity:

Sing together tonight.

Christian songs

Here are **10 beautiful Christian songs about love** — each with a short synopsis.

1. How He Loves – by John Mark McMillan

John Mark McMillan wrote this song after the tragic death of his close friend Stephen Coffey, which deeply shaped the song's message about God's overwhelming love in the middle of grief and pain.

Scripture:

The Lord hath appeared of old unto me, saying, Yea, I have loved thee with an everlasting love - **Jeremiah 31:3**

For I am persuaded, that neither death, nor life shall be able to separate us from the love of God - **Romans 8:38-39**

Synopsis:
A powerful song about God's overwhelming love—messy, deep, and relentless. It reminds us that God loves us even in our brokenness.

2. Love Came Down at Christmas – traditional hymn

by Christina Rossetti.

The words were first published in her poetry collection *Time Flies: A Reading Diary*. Later, the poem was set to music and became a beloved traditional Christmas hymn, often sung to tunes like **Gartan** or **Dominus Regit Me**.

Scripture:

For God so loved the world, that he gave his only begotten Son - **John 3:16**

And the Word was made flesh, and dwelt among us - **John 1:14**

Synopsis:
This gentle hymn celebrates Christ's birth as the greatestact of love ever given to the world.

3. The Love of God – by Frederick M. Lehman

The Love of God was written in **1917** by Frederick M. Lehman. He wrote it while working in a packing plant after losing his earlier ministry job. The famous third verse was adapted from a much older Jewish poem, believed to have been written centuries earlier and found written on the wall of an asylum room. The hymn was first published in **1917** in Lehman's collection **Songs That Are Different**.

Scripture: *Behold, what manner of love the Father hath bestowed upon us.* **1 John 3:1 (KJV)**

For God so loved the world, that he gave his only begotten Son. **John 3:16**

Synopsis:
A timeless hymn describing God's love as endless and immeasurable—greater than oceans and skies.

4. Reckless Love – by Cory Asbury

Reckless Love was released in **2017** by Cory Asbury.

It appears on his album **Reckless Love**, and he co-wrote the song with Caleb Culver and Ran Jackson. The song became widely known through Bethel Music worship.

What man of you, having an hundred sheep, if he lose one… doth not leave the ninety and nine until he find it? - **Luke 15:4**

Scripture:

But God commendeth his love toward us, in that, while we were yet sinners, Christ died for us. - **Romans 5:8**

Synopsis:
This song shows how God pursues us with unstoppable love, leaving the ninety-nine to find the one.

5. I Will Be Here – by Steven Curtis Chapman

I Will Be Here was released in **1989** by Steven Curtis Chapman.

It appears on his album **More to This Life**, and it quickly became one of his most beloved songs, especially for weddings and marriage celebrations.

Scripture:

What therefore God hath joined together, let not man put asunder. — **Matthew 19:6**

Two are better than one… for if they fall, the one will lift up his fellow. — **Ecclesiastes 4:9–10**

Synopsis:
A beautiful Christian love song about marriage vows—standing together through every storm.

6. When God Made You
– by Newsong

When God Made You was released in **2000** by the Christian group NewSong.

It appears on their album **Shelter**, and it became especially popular as a wedding and anniversary song because of its message about God bringing two people together.

Scripture:

Every good gift and every perfect gift is from above… — **James 1:17**

Synopsis:
A romantic Christian duet celebrating God's plan in bringing two people together.

7. Amazing Love (You Are My King) – by Billy James Foote

Amazing Love (You Are My King) was written in **1996** by Billy James Foote.

It became widely known through recordings by artists like Chris Tomlin and the worship collective Passion in the early 2000s.

Scripture:

Greater love hath no man than this, that a man lay down his life for his friends." — **John 15:13**

Who, being in the form of God… made himself of no reputation…" — **Philippians 2:6–8**

Synopsis:
A worship song marveling at Christ's sacrificial love and the joy of being forgiven.

8. Love Never Fails – by Brandon Heath

Love Never Fails was released in **2009** by Brandon Heath.

It appears on his album **What If We**, which also includes the well-known song *Gi*

ve Me Your Eyes.

Scripture: *Charity suffereth long, and is kind… Charity never faileth.* — **1 Corinthians 13:4, 8**

"Above all things have fervent charity among yourselves." — **1 Peter 4:8**

Synopsis:
Inspired by 1 Corinthians 13, this song reminds us that God's love outlasts everything.

9. He Knows My Name – by Francesca Battistelli

He Knows My Name was released in **2010** by Francesca Battistelli.

It appears on her album **Hundred More Years**, and the song was written by Francesca Battistelli along with Matthew West and Sam Mizell.

Scripture:

Fear thou not; for I have redeemed thee, I have called thee by thy name; thou art mine. — **Isaiah 43:1**

Synopsis:

A comforting song about God's personal love—He knows every detail of our lives.

10. God Gave Me You
– by Dave Barnes

God Gave Me You was written and released in **2010** by Dave Barnes.

It later became widely popular when recorded by Blake Shelton in **2011** on his album **Red River Blue**.

Scripture:

Whoso findeth a wife findeth a good thing, and obtaineth favour of the Lord. - **Proverbs 18:22**

Synopsis:
A romantic Christian song about gratitude for a spouse and God's blessing in marriage.

30-Day Song Companion

Thirty days of song to accompany scriptures, reflections and prayers.

DAY 1 – Love Begins with a Song

How Great Is Our God – Chris Tomlin

Why: Start love in praise to God.

DAY 2 – Singing Through Hard Times

Praise You in This Storm – Casting Crowns

Why: Faith during storms—just like Mother Rachel's strength.

DAY 3 – Love That Listens

Speak, O Lord – Keith Getty

Why: Listening hearts grow love.

DAY 4 – Faithful in Small Places

Little Is Much When God Is in It – traditional hymn

Why: God blesses small acts of love.

DAY 5 – Harmony in Marriage

I Will Be Here – Steven Curtis Chapman

Why: Marriage vows through every season.

DAY 6 – *Joy in Motherhood*

Find Your Wings – Mark Harris

Why: A mother's love guiding children.

DAY 7 – *Singing on Sundays*

Great Is Thy Faithfulness – classic hymn

Why: Worship together builds faith.

DAY 8 – *Forgiveness Restores the Song*

Forgiveness – Matthew West

Why: Forgiveness heals hearts.

DAY 9 – *Love in Loss*

It Is Well With My Soul – hymn

Why: Comfort in sorrow.

DAY 10 – *Kindness Is Music*

They'll Know We Are Christians – hymn

Why: Love shown through kindness

DAY 11 – Love That Works Hard

Do Something – Matthew West

Why: Faith in action.

DAY 12 – Singing Through the Storm

Even If – MercyMe

Why: Trust God in hardship—like that tribute band story you loved.

DAY 13 – Hope Returns

Blessed Assurance – hymn

Why: Hope in God's promises.

DAY 14 – Love Is Patient

Slow Down – Nichole Nordeman

Why: Patience in love.

DAY 15 – Celebrate Small Wins

Goodness of God – Bethel Music

Why: Thank God for little blessings

DAY 16 – Love Teaches

The Blessing – Kari Jobe

Why: Generational faith.

DAY 17 – Singing in Gratitude

Give Thanks – hymn

Why: Gratitude grows love.

DAY 18 – Love Shows Up

Here I Am, Lord – hymn

Why: Showing up for others.

DAY 19 – Love Encourages

My Story – Big Daddy Weave

Why: Encouragement through testimony.

DAY 20 – Love Is Gentle

Softly and Tenderly – hymn

Why: Gentle love.

DAY 21 – Singing in Faith

Trust in You – Lauren Daigle

Why: Trusting God's plan.

DAY 22 – Love Serves

Make Me a Servant – chorus

Why: Serving with love.

DAY 23 – Love Laughs

Joyful, Joyful, We Adore Thee – hymn

Why: Joy is holy.

DAY 24 – Love Remembers

Because He Lives – hymn

Why: Remembering God's faithfulness

DAY 25 – Love Prays Together

Sweet Hour of Prayer – hymn

Why: Prayer strengthens families.

DAY 26 – Love Trusts God

Oceans – Hillsong United

Why: Trust beyond fear.

DAY 27 – Love Persists

Press On – Building 429

Why: Keep loving without quitting.

DAY 28 – Love Comforts

I Will Carry You – Selah

Why: Comfort in grief.

DAY 29 – Love Rejoices

This Is the Day – chorus

Why: Celebrate blessings.

DAY 30 – Song for the JourneyForever

Amazing Grace – hymn

Why: God's love never ends.

Reader Guide

How to Use This Guide

You can use this book:

- Alone during quiet time
- With your spouse
- With children at bedtime
- With a women's Bible study
- With a church small group

Read one day at a time, then answer the questions below.

Weekly Reflection Questions

Reflections to accompany your Easter Journey.

Week 1 – Beginning With Praise

(Days 1–7)

1. What "song" of hope is God starting in your life?

2. What storms has your family faced together?

3. When have you felt God's comfort most?

4. How can your home become a place of praise?

Family Activity: Sing a hymn together Sunday night.

Week 2 – Love in Action

(Days 8–14)

1. Who do you need to forgive?

2. What kind words can you speak this week?

3. Where is God asking you to be patient?

4. How can you show love in small ways?

Family Activity: Write kindness notes.

Week 3 – Growing Faith

(Days 15–21)

1. What small victory can you celebrate?

2. How has motherhood or family life grown your faith?

3. What worry do you need to give to God?

4. When have you seen God answer prayer?

Family Activity: Pray together for one need.

Week 4 – Love Sings On

(Days 22–30)

1. Who needs comfort from you?

2. How can your family serve others?

3. What joyful memory reminds you of God's love?

4. What legacy of faith do you want to leave?

Family Activity: Write family gratitude list.

Pages

Write about:

1. A time love carried you through hardship

2. A person who showed you kindness

3. A prayer for your children

4. A memory of church singing together

5. One way you saw God's love this week

Couples Discussion Questions

1. What song reminds you of your relationship?

2. How can we pray together more often?

3. What stress are we carrying silently?

4. How can we encourage each other daily?

Mother & Child Activity Page

1. Sing a lullaby together

2. Pray before bed

3. Write "3 things we thank God for"

4. Draw a picture of your family singing

Group Discussion Questions

1. Which devotion touched you most?

2. What verse spoke to your heart?

3. How did your prayer life change?

4. What habit will you continue?

Closing Prayer

Lord, let love sing in our homes.
Teach us kindness, patience, and faith.
Help our families grow closer to You.
Let our lives be songs of hope.
Amen.

Leader's Guide

This study helps church groups:

- Grow closer to Jesus
- Strengthen marriages and families
- Encourage one another through hard seasons
- Build prayer habits
- Create loving Christian community

Each meeting focuses on **one week of devotionals**.

Leader Preparation Checklist

Before each meeting:

1. Pray for each member by name

2. Read the week's devotionals

3. Choose one song to play

4. Prepare discussion questions

5. Plan closing prayer

Keep meetings warm, gentle, and hopeful.

Suggested Group Format (60–75 Minutes)

1. Opening prayer – 5 min

2. Worship song – 5 min

3. Scripture reading – 5 min

4. Discussion – 30 min

5. Prayer requests – 15 min

6. Closing prayer – 5 min

Week-by-Week Leader Plans

Week 1 – Love Begins With Praise (Days 1–7)

Scripture Focus:

Psalm 95:1

Discussion Questions:

1. What does "love sings on" mean in your life?

2. When have you seen God carry your family?

3. What praise habit can you start this week?

4. What storms are you facing now?

Activity:

Sing a hymn together.

Suggested Song:
Great Is Thy Faithfulness

Week 2 – Love in Action (Days 8–14)

Scripture Focus:

Ephesians 4:32

Discussion Questions:

1. Why is forgiveness difficult?

2. How can we show kindness daily?

3. What does patience look like in marriage or parenting?

4. Who needs encouragement this week?

Activity:

Write encouragement notes.

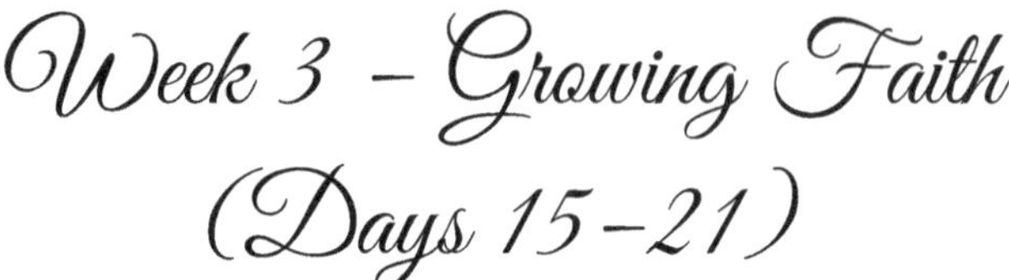

Week 3 – Growing Faith (Days 15–21)

Scripture Focus:

Proverbs 3:5

Discussion Questions:

1. What small victory did you celebrate?

2. Where do you struggle to trust God?

3. How has motherhood or family life grown your faith?

4. What prayer was answered recently?

Activity:

Pray in pairs.

Week 4 – Song for the Journey Forever (Days 22–30)

Scripture Focus:

Psalm 89:1

Discussion Questions:

1. What legacy of faith do you want to leave?

2. How can our church show love to hurting families?

3. What memory reminds you of God's faithfulness?

4. How will you keep a daily devotional habit?

Activity:

Create a gratitude list.

Leader Tips for Success

1. Encourage quiet members gently

2. Avoid correcting personal stories

3. Keep conversation hopeful

4. Share Scripture often

5. Pray together sincerely

Remember—people come to be comforted, not impressed.

Prayer Ideas for Leaders

1. For marriages

2. For mothers

3. For grieving families

4. For children and teens

5. For church unity

Optional Activities

1. Sing a hymn night

2. Write prayer cards

3. Bake cookies together

4. Deliver meals to a family

5. Invite testimonies

These build community beautifully.

Closing Blessing

May the Lord bless your group with kindness.
May your homes be filled with prayer.
May your faith grow stronger together.
And may love sing on in every heart.

Amen.

Songs for the Journey: Faith That Keeps Singing

Sermon 1 – When Love Begins With Praise

Scripture:

Psalm 95:1
"O come, let us sing unto the Lord…"

Main Idea:

The strongest love stories start with praise.

Points:

1. Praise before the storm comes

2. Praise during hardship

3. Praise after deliverance

Illustration:

A faithful couple singing together through trials—like your Haven Ridge families.

Closing Prayer:

Lord, teach our homes to sing in gratitude.

Sermon 2 – Singing Through the Storm

Scripture:

Psalm 30:5
"Weeping may endure for a night…"

Main Idea:

Faithful love survives storms.

Points:

1. Storms are part of every journey

2. God stays present in suffering

3. Joy returns in God's timing

Application:

Encourage couples and families facing illness, grief, or stress.

Sermon 3 – Love That Listens

Scripture:

James 1:19
"Swift to hear, slow to speak..."

Main Idea:

Listening is an act of love.

Points:

1. God listens to us

2. We must listen to family

3. Listening heals wounds

Application:

Marriage and parenting counseling message.

Sermon 4 – Faithful in Small Places

Scripture:

Luke 16:10
"He that is faithful in that which is least…"

Main Idea:

God blesses ordinary faithfulness.

Points:

1. Small acts build strong homes

2. Daily kindness matters

3. Hidden faith grows big fruit

Illustration:

Mothers praying at night, fathers working faithfully.

Sermon 5 – Forgiveness Restores the Song

Scripture:

Ephesians 4:32
"Be ye kind… forgiving one another…"

Main Idea:

Forgiveness heals families.

Points:

1. Hurt is inevitable

2. Bitterness destroys love

3. Forgiveness restores peace

Application:

Encourage reconciliation.

Sermon 6 – Song for the Journey Forever

Scripture:

Psalm 89:1
"I will sing of the mercies of the Lord for ever…"

Main Idea:

God's love never ends.

Points:

1. Love outlives hardship

2. Faith becomes legacy

3. Heaven completes the song

Application:

Encourage hope after loss.

Optional Sermon Topics

1. Joy in Motherhood – Proverbs 31:28

2. Trusting God – Proverbs 3:5

3. Comforting the Grieving – 2 Corinthians 1:4

4. Celebrating Small Victories – Zechariah 4:10

5. Singing in Gratitude – 1 Thessalonians 5:18

Series Closing Prayer

Lord, let love sing in our homes.
Strengthen marriages and families.
Comfort hurting hearts.
Keep our faith strong until we sing with You in heaven.
Amen.

Song for the Journey– Kids Messages

1. Love Begins With a Song

Scripture:

Psalm 95:1
"O come, let us sing unto the Lord…"

Message:

Have you ever sung your favorite song?

When we sing to God, it tells Him we love Him.
Families that sing together stay strong.

Lesson:

Love starts with praising God.

Prayer:

Dear Jesus, help our hearts sing to You. Amen.

Activity:

Sing one hymn together.

2. Singing Through Hard Times

Scripture:

Psalm 30:5
"Weeping may endure for a night…"

Message:

Sometimes we feel sad.
Maybe a toy breaks. Maybe someone is sick.

But God brings joy again—like sunshine after rain.

Lesson:

Keep trusting God when life is hard.

Prayer:

Jesus, help us trust You when we are sad. Amen.

Activity:

Draw rain clouds and sunshine.

3. Love Listens

Scripture:

James 1:19
"Swift to hear, slow to speak…"

Message:

Listening shows love.

When Mom talks… listen.
When your friend is sad… listen.

Jesus listens to us too.

Lesson:

Listening is loving.

Prayer:

Help me listen kindly, Jesus.

Activity:

Play the "quiet listening" game.

4. Faithful in Small Things

Scripture

Luke 16:10

Message:

Big love grows from little chores.

Cleaning toys… helping dishes… sharing snacks.

These are songs of love.

Lesson:

Small kindness matters.

Prayer:

Help me do little things with love.

Activity:

Pick one chore to help with today.

5. Forgiveness Restores Love

Scripture:

Ephesians 4:32

Message:

Sometimes we hurt each other.

When we say "I'm sorry," love comes back.

Like fixing a broken toy.

Lesson:

Forgiveness heals hearts.

Prayer:

Jesus, help me forgive.

Activity:

Write a sorry note.

6. Song for the Journey Forever

Scripture:

Psalm 89:1
"I will sing of the mercies of the Lord for ever…"

Message:

God's love never stops.

Even when we grow up… even in heaven…
God keeps loving us.

Lesson:

God's love lasts forever.

Prayer:

Thank You for loving me always.

Activity:

Draw your family singing together.

Leader Tips for Children's Sermons

1. Keep it under 7 minutes

2. Use props (toy, umbrella, music box)

3. Let kids answer questions

4. End with singing

Kids LOVE singing.

Through loss and waiting, through illness and uncertainty, God's promise still sings over us: "Weeping may endure for a night, but joy cometh in the morning."
—Psalm 30:5

Joy returns.

And through every season of life, we remember: "I will sing of the mercies of the Lord for ever: with my mouth will I make known thy faithfulness to all generations."
—Psalm 89:1

God's love sings on.

This book is dedicated to the quiet heroes of faith—
the ones who forgive,
who pray,
who keep loving,
who hold families together when life feels fragile.

 May the Lord bless you and keep you.

May He fill your home with peace.

May He strengthen your heart with hope. And may your life become a song of love that never ends.

With gratitude and prayer,

Karen Kazimer Shockley

About The Author

Karen Kazimer Shockley

Karen Kazimer Shockley is a passionate author who has touched the hearts of readers with her inspiring books centered on celebrating holidays, heartfelt romances, and uplifting stories about Christianity.

Her works beautifully weave together faith, love, and the joy of special moments, creating stories that resonate with readers of all ages.

Visit her website at www.karenswords.com

Daily Devotionals for Every Season

Life is a journey—sometimes joyful, sometimes difficult, always guided by God's faithful love.

In the Journey Series, inspirational author Karen Kazimer Shockley offers warm, Scripture-centered devotionals rooted in the King James Version of the Bible, written for mothers, families, home-schoolers, pastors, and everyday believers seeking strength and encouragement.

Each book in the series provides:

Daily KJV Scripture readings

Heartfelt devotionals drawn from real life and biblical truth

Practical faith lessons for home, work, and ministry

Prayers and reflection questions

Activities and journaling prompts

Whether you need courage for today, grace for tomorrow, or joy for the road ahead, these devotionals will walk beside you—helping you grow closer to God one day at a time.

Perfect for personal quiet time, small groups, gifts for friends, or family devotions.

Books in the Journey Series include:

• Song for the Journey – Finding hope through daily praise

• Wisdom for the Journey – 30 Days of Biblical Leadership

• Strength for the Journey – Courage for life's hard seasons

• Grace for the Journey – Living with compassion and faith

• Joy for the Journey – Celebrating God's goodness each day

Walk the journey with God—and discover peace, purpose, and lasting hope.

Strength For The Journey

Being a man today isn't easy. This is especially true for fathers. The world tells you to chase success, hide weakness, and measure your worth by what you achieve. But God calls you to something greater—courage, character, faith, and love.

This 30-day devotional is designed to help you walk that path. Each day includes:

Scripture to guide your thoughts
Reflection to challenge and encourage you
Prayer to connect you with God's strength
Challenges to strengthen your faith

Whether you're just beginning your walk with Christ or have walked with Him for decades, this journey will encourage you to:

Live with integrity, even when no one is watching
Lead with humility, courage, and wisdom
Build a faith that can weather every storm
Leave behind a legacy of godliness that impacts generations

Take 5–10 minutes a day. Grab your Bible, quiet your heart, and let God's Word renew your strength.

This isn't just about being a good man and a good father—it's about becoming a Godly one.

Your strength matters. Your influence matters.

Your journey starts now.

Love For The Journey: 30 Days Of Scripture, Prayer And Purpose

What if 30 days could change the way you love—and the way you feel loved?

Love isn't just an emotion. It's a calling. A daily choice. A reflection of the heart of God.

In Love Fully: 30 Days of Scripture, Prayer & Purposethoughts, heartfelt prayers, and simple daily activities to help you live out God's greatest commandment—to love Him and others.
Whether you're feeling spiritually dry, emotionally tired, or simply longing to grow deeper in your faith, this devotional is your invitation to slow down and soak in the truth of God's unchanging love for you.

Perfect for personal study, small groups, or gift-giving, this book will remind you that:

You are seen, known, and cherished by your Creator.
Love is not something you earn—it's something you receive and reflect.
Small acts of love, rooted in faith, can change your heart and your home.

Let God's love transform your life—one verse, one prayer, one beautiful day at a time.

Wisdom For The Journey

Lead with courage. Serve with grace. Grow in God.
What does true leadership look like in a world hungry for integrity, compassion, and faith?
In Wisdom for the Journey: 30 Days of Biblical Leadership, best-selling inspirational author Karen Kazimer Shockley invites you into a powerful 30-day devotional rooted in the King James Version of the Bible, designed to help you lead with Christlike wisdom —at home, at work, in church, and in your community.
Whether you're a parent guiding your children, a teacher shaping young minds, a pastor shepherding a flock, or a team leader seeking God's direction, this devotional will help you walk confidently in the calling God has placed on your life.
Each day includes:
✓ A carefully chosen KJV Scripture on leadership

✓ A heartfelt devotional with real-life and biblical examples
✓ A practical leadership principle you can apply immediately
✓ A reflection question for deeper growth
✓ A closing prayer to strengthen your faith

Grace For The Journey

You are seen. You are strong. You are deeply loved.

In the everyday moments of motherhood—where laundry piles up, sleep is scarce, and love is poured out in countless quiet ways—it's easy to feel overwhelmed or overlooked. But God sees you, and He is with you in every moment.

This 30-day devotional is a heartfelt companion for mothers in all seasons of life. Each day features
- a powerful Scripture from the King James Version,
- a thoughtful devotional reflection
- a heartfelt prayer, and
- a simple, meaningful activity

designed to help you grow in faith, find peace in the chaos, and rediscover the beauty of your calling.

Whether you're a new mom, a seasoned parent, or somewhere in between, this devotional will encourage your soul, strengthen your spirit, and remind you of this truth: you are never alone—and your work as a mother has eternal significance.

Perfect gift for mothers

www.ingramcontent.com/pod-product-compliance
Lightning Source LLC
Chambersburg PA
CBHW051808050726
47598CB00006B/2467